SAINSBURY'S

Quick and Easy
Food for Friends

Lesley Waters

Contents

Published exclusively for J Sainsbury plc
Stamford House Stamford Street
London SE1 9LL
by Martin Books
Simon & Schuster Consumer Group
Grafton House 64 Maids Causeway
Cambridge CB5 8DD

Published 1995
ISBN 0 85941 885 5
© 1995 Martin Books

Printed and bound in the UK by Bath Press Colourbooks
Design: Green Moore Lowenhoff
Photography: Steve Baxter
Styling: Jane McLeish
Food preparation: Jane Stevenson
Typesetting: Stylize

Pictured on the front cover: Cod Cassoulet (page 22)

Introduction

Cooking for friends can be an extremely satisfying experience, but few of us have the leisure to spend hours planning or cooking an elaborate meal. Still, it is nice to have people over, and nicer still when you can offer them something a bit special.

The recipes in this book are aimed at informal entertaining – the kind of quick-and-easy meals you can put together at the end of a busy workday, or even when people drop by unexpectedly and you have to reach way into the back of your storecupboard. There are suggestions and recipes for all kinds of casual gatherings – drinks and nibbles, intimate suppers, and even cooking for a crowd.

With a helpful storecupboard checklist and tips on how to personalise ready-prepared foods, this book should be a useful guide for the not-so-confident cook as well as inspiring the experienced host to try a new style of entertaining.

So whether you've invited the neighbours over for a spur-of-the-moment Sunday brunch, or you're hosting a more elaborate buffet party, you should find some recipes to suit, and the confidence to entertain with style and flair. Best of all, you'll be able to spend your time talking to your guests instead of to your kitchen wall!

KITCHEN UTENSILS AND APPLIANCES

Although there are many labour-saving kitchen devices which can save you both time and energy, there are very few items which can be deemed essential. The only electric appliance that is called for in these recipes is the ever-useful food processor or liquidiser. Otherwise, this is my list of necessary kitchen aids:

a few sharp knives
a knife sharpener
a wok
a large non-stick frying pan
a good balloon whisk
wooden spoons

a spatula
large metal spoons
a palette knife or good fish slice
baking or roasting trays
chopping boards
a corkscrew

THE STORECUPBOARD

A well-stocked storecupboard or larder allows you to be more creative and spontaneous in the kitchen. It will also save you from those otherwise inevitable last-minute trips to the shops before your guests arrive! To build up your storecupboard and freezer, just buy one or two extra items each week. This will prevent a sudden increase in your grocery bill and get you in the habit of noticing interesting ingredients in your super-market that may come in handy later on.

CANS, CARTONS AND JARS:

antipasto – artichokes, mushrooms, peppers
beans – black-eyed, butter, flageolet, pinto, red kidney, black kidney, cannellini
chopped tomatoes
coconut milk
fruit – apricots, mandarins, pears, plums
lumpfish roe
morello cherries
new potatoes
passata (creamed tomatoes)
peanut butter
olives – black and green
red pimentos
red salmon
sun-dried tomatoes
UHT milk
UHT cream

DRIED FRUITS, NUTS AND SEEDS:

desiccated coconut
dried mushrooms
fruits – apricots, dates, prunes, raisins, sultanas
nuts – flaked almonds, pine kernels, pistachios, walnuts
seeds – poppy, sesame

FLAVOURINGS AND SPICES:

beer
black bean sauce
chilli sauce
cocoa powder
continental plain chocolate
curry paste
dried herbs – bay leaves, dill seeds, mixed herbs, oregano, sage, thyme
dried spices – cardamom, cayenne pepper, chilli powder, cinnamon, coriander, curry powder, cumin, garam masala, nutmeg, paprika, turmeric, garlic
mustards – Dijon, German, coarse-grained
oils – olive, sesame, sunflower
olive paste
pesto sauce
sea salt
soy sauce
stock cubes
sugar – brown, caster, demerara, icing, white
sun-dried tomato paste
vanilla essence
vinegars – balsamic, cider, wine
wine
Worcestershire sauce

GRAINS AND PULSES AND BAKING PRODUCTS:

baking powder
Basmati rice
dried pasta
green lentils
instant polenta
long-grain rice (easy-cook)
oatmeal
pearl barley
plain flour
porridge oats
powdered gelatine
red lentils
risotto rice

FREEZER:

bacon
butter
chicken and poultry
filo pastry
fish fillets
frozen peas
ice cream
mince
puff pastry
stewing beef
summer fruits

RECIPE NOTES

All recipes in this book give ingredients in both metric (g, ml, etc.) and imperial (oz, pints, etc.) measures. Use either set of quantities, but not a mixture of both, in any one recipe.

All teaspoons and tablespoons are level, unless otherwise stated.
1 teaspoon = a 5 ml spoon;
1 tablespoon = a 15 ml spoon.

Egg size is medium (size 3), unless otherwise stated.

Vegetables and fruit are medium-size unless otherwise stated.

Freshly ground black pepper should be used throughout.

PREPARATION AND COOKING TIMES

Preparation and cooking times are included at the head of the recipes as a general guide; preparation times, especially, are approximate and timings are usually rounded to the nearest 5 minutes.

Preparation times include the time taken to prepare ingredients in the list, but not to make any 'basic' recipe.

The cooking times given at the heads of the recipes denote cooking periods when the dish can be left largely unattended, e.g. baking, and not the total amount of cooking time for the recipe. Always read and follow the timings given for the steps of the recipe in the method.

Nibbles and Tapas

These quick and terribly easy mouthwatering morsels are great to munch on with a drink while dinner is cooking. If you prepare a selection they can be served as tapas or as a first course.

Green and Black Olives in Pistou

Preparation and cooking time: 10 minutes + marinating. Freezing: not recommended. Serves 4–6.

These delicious nibbles are child's play to make.

250 g (8 oz) jar Greek-style olives, drained
300 g (10 oz) jar green olives, drained
1 packet fresh basil
3 tablespoons chopped fresh parsley

4 garlic cloves, crushed
6 tablespoons olive oil
salt and freshly ground black pepper

❶ Combine the olives in a mixing bowl.
❷ Using a food processor or liquidiser, blend together the basil, parsley, garlic and olive oil, and season well.

❸ Pour the pistou over the olives and toss well to coat. Transfer to a serving dish and leave to marinate at room temperature for 30 minutes.

Salami Bites

Preparation and cooking time: 10 minutes + chilling. Freezing: not recommended. Makes 12–16 pieces.

These bite-sized wedges are the perfect savoury snack to make when friends pop by for a drink.

150 g (5 oz) cream cheese
2 shallots, chopped finely
2 tablespoons capers, chopped
2 tablespoons chopped fresh tarragon
  or parsley

10 slices round pepper salami
salt and freshly ground black pepper
watercress, to garnish

❶ Combine the cream cheese, shallots, capers and tarragon or parsley together and season well.
❷ Sandwich 5 slices of salami together with layers of the cream cheese mixture.

Wrap in clingfilm and refrigerate. Repeat with the remaining 5 slices of salami.
❸ Cut each chilled salami round in 6–8 wedges and serve on a platter, garnished with some watercress.

Brie and Grape Crostini

Preparation and cooking time: 15 minutes.
Freezing: not recommended. Makes about 20.

You can make the bread croûtes ahead and pop them in the oven
once your guests arrive. Few will be able to resist the combination
of creamy melted Brie and sweet grapes, warm from the oven.

1 thin french stick
2 tablespoons olive oil
250 g (8 oz) Brie, sliced

250 g (8 oz) mixed red and green seedless
  grapes
freshly ground black pepper

❶ Preheat the oven to Gas Mark 6/200°C/
400°F.
❷ Cut the french stick in 1 cm (¹/₂-inch)
slices and brush them with the olive oil.
Bake for 10 minutes and then leave to
cool. Keep the oven on.

❸ Top each croûte with a slice of cheese,
and push 2 grapes into each. Season with
black pepper.
❹ Place the croûtes on a baking tray and
heat through for 10 minutes. Leave to
cool slightly before serving.

Pepper Crostini

Preparation and cooking time: 10 minutes.
Freezing: not recommended. Makes about 20.

These pepper crostini won't stay on the platter for long. Just double
the quantities for larger parties.

1 thin french stick
2 tablespoons olive oil
200 ml (7 fl oz) crème fraîche

400 g (13 oz) antipasto peppers, drained
salt and freshly ground black pepper
basil leaves, to garnish

❶ Preheat the oven to Gas Mark 6/200°C/
400°F.
❷ Cut the french stick in 1 cm (¹/₂-inch)
slices and brush them with the olive oil.
Bake for 10 minutes and then leave to
cool.

❸ Season the crème fraîche with salt and
pepper and spoon it on to the crostini.
Top with the drained peppers, decorate
with basil leaves and serve.

Sesame Sausages with Apple and Mustard Dip

Preparation and cooking time: 25 minutes.
Freezing: not recommended. Serves 4–6.

You'll need cocktail sticks to serve these tasty sausage titbits.

500 g (1 lb) cocktail sausages or chipolatas
    cut in 5 cm (2-inch) lengths
2 tablespoons clear honey
3 tablespoons soy sauce
2 tablespoons sesame seeds
freshly ground black pepper

For the dip:
4 tablespoons mayonnaise
1½ tablespoons coarse-grained mustard
1 dessert apple, grated
freshly ground black pepper

❶ Preheat the oven to Gas Mark 6/200°C/400°F.

❷ Place the sausages on a baking tray and season well with pepper. Bake for 10–15 minutes and then drain off any excess fat.

❸ Combine the honey, soy sauce and sesame seeds in a small bowl. Pour this over the sausages and return them to the oven for 6–8 minutes, until the sausages are glazed and the sesame seeds are golden brown.

❹ Meanwhile, mix together the dip ingredients and season to taste with pepper. Transfer the dip to a serving dish and serve alongside the sesame sausages with some cocktail sticks to aid dipping.

Dried Fruit and Spiced Nut Platter

Preparation and cooking time: 10 minutes.
Freezing: not recommended. Serves 4–6.

This makes a tasty and healthy alternative to the usual bowl of crisps and nuts. You could replace the dried fruits with fresh dates.

500 g (1 lb) shelled whole nuts (e.g., brazils,
    walnut halves, pecans etc.)
1 tablespoon olive oil
1 teaspoon chilli powder
1 teaspoon ground coriander

1 teaspoon cumin
salt and freshly ground black pepper
selection of dried fruits (e.g., dates, prunes,
    apricots, figs etc.), to garnish

❶ Preheat the oven to Gas Mark 6/200°C/400°F.

❷ Scatter the nuts in a shallow roasting tin and sprinkle them with oil and spices. Season and toss well to coat. Cook them for 6–8 minutes, or until lightly roasted, stirring occasionally.

❸ Allow the nuts to cool and then transfer them to a shallow serving dish, set on a platter or basket. Surround the dish with dried fruits and serve.

Salmon and Lime Pâté

Preparation and cooking time: 10 minutes.
Freezing: not recommended. Serves 4–6.

This fresh-tasting pâté is breathtakingly quick to make using a food processor. Serve it with fresh vegetables or a selection of warm sesame crackers and taco chips. Either way, it's sure to be a hit.

418 g can of red salmon, drained
175 g (6 oz) herb and garlic flavoured soft
  cheese
2 tablespoons Greek-style yogurt

grated zest and juice of 2 limes
2 teaspoons olive oil
1 tablespoon chopped fresh parsley
freshly ground black pepper

❶ Combine the salmon, cheese, yogurt and lime zest and juice in a food processor or liquidiser. Blend until just smooth and season to taste with pepper.
❷ Transfer the pâté to a serving dish. Drizzle the olive oil over and sprinkle with the parsley.

❸ Arrange the dish on a large platter or basket and surround with freshly cut vegetables, warm sesame crackers or taco chips.

Spicy Hot Potatoes

Preparation and cooking time: 25–30 minutes.
Freezing: not recommended. Serves 4.

These spicy potato gems could be served as a cocktail party snack. Just pierce each one with a toothpick for easy handling and watch them disappear!

500 g (1 lb) small new potatoes
2 tablespoons olive oil
1 garlic clove, crushed
2 teaspoons chilli powder

6 tablespoons tomato passata
2 large ripe tomatoes, chopped
juice of 1 lemon
salt and freshly ground black pepper

❶ Cook the potatoes in lightly salted boiling water for about 12 minutes, or until just tender. Preheat the oven to Gas Mark 6/200°C/400°F.
❷ Meanwhile, heat 1 tablespoon of the oil in a small saucepan and quickly sauté the garlic and chilli powder. Add the passata, chopped tomatoes and lemon juice and season well. Simmer for 6–7 minutes and then set aside.

❸ Drain the potatoes and place them in a shallow roasting pan. Drizzle the remaining olive oil over them and season well. Toss gently to coat and roast for 8 minutes, until golden.
❹ Toss the roasted potatoes in the spicy tomato sauce and serve warm.

Oriental Chicken with Coconut Sauce

Preparation and cooking time: 20 minutes + marinating. Freezing: not recommended. Serves 4–6.

The contrast of sweet and spicy flavours has an Eastern appeal.

2 skinless chicken breasts, cut in 10 pieces
coriander leaves, to garnish
For the marinade:
juice of 2 limes
2 teaspoons clear honey
1 green chilli, chopped finely
3 teaspoons sesame oil
2.5 cm (1-inch) piece of fresh root
   ginger, grated

salt and freshly ground black pepper
For the sauce:
4 spring onions, chopped
1 tablespoon sesame oil
300 ml (1/2 pint) coconut milk
150 ml (1/4 pint) vegetable stock
1 tablespoon lime pickle
1 tablespoon chopped fresh coriander

1 Combine the marinade ingredients in a shallow dish and leave the chicken to marinate for at least 30 minutes.

2 Meanwhile, mix together the sauce ingredients in a saucepan and simmer gently for 10–12 minutes. Set aside.

3 Stir-fry the chicken with the marinade for 8–10 minutes until cooked through.

4 Thread the cooked chicken pieces on to bamboo skewers, alternating them with the coriander leaves. Serve on a platter with the coconut sauce alongside.

Mushroom Morsels in Coriander

Preparation time: 10 minutes + 2 hours marinating. Freezing: not recommended. Serves 4–6.

Serve this dish as a first course accompanied by warm, crusty bread.

500 g (1 lb) button mushrooms, wiped
grated zest of 1 lemon
chopped fresh parsley, to garnish
For the dressing:
2 tablespoons coriander seeds, crushed
3 tablespoons lemon juice

6 tablespoons olive oil
2 teaspoons Dijon mustard
1 tablespoon water
a pinch of sugar
salt and freshly ground black pepper

1 Put the mushrooms in a large bowl.

2 Blend the dressing ingredients together and season well. Pour over the mushrooms. Toss gently to coat and leave to marinate at room temperature for 2 hours.

3 Transfer the mushrooms with their juices to a serving dish. Mix together the lemon zest and parsley and scatter over the mushrooms. Serve at once.

Entertaining from your Storecupboard

Although the idea of the storecupboard or larder may sound old fashioned, it is the lifesaver of today's busy cook. Keep it well-stocked and it will save you time and trouble in the long run. And don't forget that the refrigerator and freezer can also be used to store many basic ingredients, making your life easier than ever. See the storecupboard section (pages 4–5) to get some ideas for your own kitchen.

Red Salmon Fishcakes with Real Tartare Sauce

Preparation and cooking time: 25 minutes.
Freezing: not recommended. Serves 4.

Canned red salmon has a good strong flavour which works well for fishcakes. Try serving them with buttered petit pois, seasoned with freshly ground nutmeg and black pepper.

418 g can of red salmon
500 g (1 lb) mashed potatoes
1 small onion, peeled and grated
2 tablespoons capers, chopped
grated zest and juice of 1 lemon or lime
1 egg, size 1, beaten
200 g (7 oz) dried breadcrumbs
sunflower oil for shallow-frying
lemon or lime wedges, to serve
salt and freshly ground black pepper

For the tartare sauce:
1 small onion, peeled and grated
3 tablespoons capers, chopped
5 tablespoons mayonnaise
2 tablespoons fromage frais or Greek-style yogurt
2 tablespoons chopped fresh parsley
1 tablespoon chopped fresh tarragon (optional)
lemon or lime juice to taste
salt and freshly ground black pepper

❶ Flake the salmon into a mixing bowl, discarding any skin and bones. Stir in the mashed potatoes, grated onion, capers, and lemon or lime zest and juice. Season to taste and mix well.

❷ Shape the mixture in 8 large fishcakes and place them on a baking tray. Place in the freezer to chill for 8–10 minutes.

❸ Meanwhile, blend together the sauce ingredients and transfer to a serving dish. Set aside.

❹ Remove the fishcakes from the freezer and brush them with the beaten egg. Coat them all over with the breadcrumbs and shallow-fry them for 3–4 minutes on each side, until golden brown. Drain on kitchen paper.

❺ Serve the fishcakes hot with the tartare sauce, garnished with lemon or lime wedges.

Pasta with Pine Kernels and Rich Mushroom Sauce

Preparation and cooking time: 30 minutes.
Freezing: not recommended. Serves 4.

Dried mushrooms impart an intense flavour to sauces.

50 g (2 oz) dried mushrooms
600 ml (1 pint) boiling water
2 tablespoons olive oil
2 large onions, sliced finely
1 teaspoon dried oregano
1 bay leaf
1 level tablespoon flour
150 ml (¼ pint) red wine or beer
150 ml (¼ pint) vegetable stock

400 g (13 oz) can of red pimentos, drained
and sliced
salt and freshly ground black pepper
For the pasta:
375 g (12 oz) linguini, tagliatelle or spaghetti
1 tablespoon olive oil
125 g (4 oz) pine kernels
75 g (3 oz) parmesan cheese, grated
salt and freshly ground black pepper

❶ Cover the dried mushrooms with boiling water and set aside to soak.

❷ Meanwhile, heat the olive oil in a saucepan and sauté the onions until softened. Add the oregano, bay leaf and flour and cook for 1 minute. Pour in the wine or beer and stock and bring to a boil, stirring until smooth. Add the mushrooms and water and simmer for 15–20 minutes. Season well. Add the pimentos 5 minutes before serving.

❸ Meanwhile, cook the pasta according to the pack instructions and drain well. Heat the olive oil in a saucepan and stir in the pine kernels, drained pasta, parmesan cheese and salt and pepper. Toss well and serve at once with the mushroom sauce.

Artichoke Frittata

Preparation and cooking time: 20 minutes.
Freezing: not recommended. Serves 4.

This quick-and-easy dish is ideal for unexpected supper guests.

2 tablespoons olive oil
2 large onions, sliced
2 garlic cloves, crushed
400 g (13 oz) can of artichoke hearts,
drained and quartered

540 g can of new potatoes, drained
and sliced
5 eggs, size 1
75 g (3 oz) Roquefort cheese, crumbled
salt and freshly ground black pepper

❶ Heat the oil in a large frying pan and gently sauté the onions until softened.

❷ Add the garlic, artichoke hearts and sliced potatoes and fry for 2 minutes more. Season well.

❸ Beat the eggs in a mixing bowl and season well. Pour into the frying pan, reduce the heat and cook gently for 4–5 minutes. Preheat the grill.

❹ Scatter the cheese on top and slide the pan under the grill until the top is golden brown and set. Serve immediately.

Cheesy Polenta with Pea and Tomato Ragoût

Preparation and cooking time: 30 minutes.
Freezing: not recommended. Serves 4.

No need to go on a special shopping trip for this recipe as you'll likely find all the ingredients in your fridge or cupboards already.

375 g (12 oz) instant polenta
2 garlic cloves, crushed
175 g (6 oz) mature Cheddar cheese, grated
125 g (4 oz) parmesan cheese, grated
freshly ground nutmeg
salt and freshly ground black pepper
For the ragoût sauce:
1 tablespoon olive oil
1 large onion, chopped
4 rashers lean smoked bacon, diced

1 large cooking apple, peeled, cored
    and chopped
400 g (13 oz) can of chopped tomatoes
550 g jar of tomato passata (creamed
    tomatoes)
1 bay leaf
2 teaspoons dried thyme
125 g (4 oz) frozen peas
salt and freshly ground black pepper

❶ Make the ragoût sauce. Heat the oil in a saucepan and fry the onion and bacon until golden brown. Stir in the chopped apple and fry for 3 minutes more. Add the chopped tomatoes, passata, bay leaf and thyme. Season well and bring to a boil. Simmer for 15 minutes, add the peas and simmer for 5 minutes more.

❷ Meanwhile, cook the polenta according to the packet instructions, seasoning well. Preheat the grill and mix the garlic, half of the grated cheese and the nutmeg in with the cooked polenta.

❸ Transfer the polenta to a greased, flameproof dish, scatter with the remaining cheese and place under the grill for 6–8 minutes, until bubbling hot and golden. Serve at once with the ragoût sauce.

Cod Cassoulet

Preparation and cooking time: 25 minutes.
Freezing: not recommended. Serves 4.

You can use frozen salmon, hoki or plaice fillets instead of cod or haddock in this recipe. Each will add their own subtle flavour to the tomato and herb base.

6 rashers smoked lean bacon, chopped
750 g (1½ lb) frozen cod or haddock fillets,
   skinned and thawed
a handful of large lettuce or spinach leaves,
   washed and patted dry
400 g (13 oz) can of chopped tomatoes
250 ml (8 fl oz) tomato passata
1 tablespoon sun-dried tomato paste
2 large tomatoes, chopped roughly

a large sprig of thyme
420 g can of butter beans, drained
420 g can of borlotti beans, drained
freshly ground black pepper
For the topping (optional):
125 g (4 oz) dried breadcrumbs
75 g (3 oz) parmesan or mature Cheddar
   cheese, grated

❶ Dry-fry the bacon in a large, non-stick pan.

❷ Cut the fish fillets in half and wrap each half in a lettuce or spinach leaf. Place them in the pan on top of the bacon.

❸ Mix the canned tomatoes with the passata and tomato paste, and season well with pepper. Pour the tomato mixture over the fish and scatter the fresh chopped tomatoes, thyme and canned beans on top.

❹ Cover the frying pan with a lid or kitchen foil. Bring to a boil and simmer for 6–8 minutes.

❺ If you wish, mix together the breadcrumbs and grated cheese. Preheat the grill. Scatter the breadcrumb mixture over the fish and place the pan under the grill, making sure to protect the handle from the flames. Grill until the topping is bubbling and golden. Serve immediately.

Spiced Turmeric Chicken

Preparation and cooking time: 45 minutes.
Freezing: not recommended. Serves 4.

This aromatic chicken dish is best served with Basmati rice. You could also try it with steamed potatoes tossed in chilli oil, black pepper and fresh mint – delicious!

2 tablespoons sunflower oil

3 large onions, sliced finely

2 garlic cloves, crushed

3 teaspoons turmeric

2 teaspoons garam masala

8 frozen chicken thighs or pieces, thawed
  and skinned

600 ml (1 pint) vegetable stock

juice of 1 lemon

1 bay leaf

142 ml (5 fl oz) double cream

2 tablespoons ground almonds

salt and freshly ground black pepper

To serve:

2 tablespoons chopped fresh mint

25 g (1 oz) toasted slivered almonds

❶ Heat the oil in a large, covered frying pan and gently fry the onions until they are softened and beginning to brown.

❷ Add the garlic, turmeric and garam masala and sauté for 1 minute. Add the chicken pieces and cook for 4 minutes more, turning the chicken frequently.

❸ Pour in the stock, lemon juice and bay leaf. Season well, cover and simmer gently for 30–35 minutes, or until the chicken is cooked through. Add extra liquid if the chicken becomes dry.

❹ Add the cream, ground almonds and half of the chopped mint, and simmer for 2 minutes more. Season to taste and transfer to a warm serving dish. Sprinkle with the remaining chopped mint and the toasted almonds and serve immediately.

Morello Cherry Ganache with Vanilla Ice Cream

Preparation and cooking time: 10 minutes.
Freezing: not recommended. Serves 4.

This simple dessert is truly scrumptious. Use a premium ice cream and make it extra special.

680 g jar morello cherries
175 g (6 oz) deluxe plain cooking chocolate, chopped roughly

2 tablespoons dark rum (optional)
vanilla ice cream, to serve

❶ Pour the cherries and their juices into a medium-sized saucepan. Add the chopped chocolate and heat gently, stirring constantly until the chocolate has melted. Simmer for a minute and stir in the rum (if using). Set aside to cool slightly.

❷ Spoon the ice cream into large glasses and pour the warm cherry ganache over. Serve at once.

Warm Walnut Plum Pavlova

Preparation and cooking time: 40 minutes.
Freezing: not recommended. Serves 4.

Warm pavlovas topped with fromage frais and plums – delicious! You can substitute any fresh or canned fruit for the plums.

3 egg whites
175 g (6 oz) caster sugar
125 g (4 oz) walnuts, chopped
1 teaspoon cornflour
1/2 teaspoon vinegar

375 g (12 oz) fromage frais or Greek-style yogurt
567 g can of red plums, drained and stoned

❶ Preheat the oven to Gas Mark 5/190°C/375°F. Line a baking tray with non-stick baking parchment.

❷ In a large, spotlessly clean bowl, whisk the egg whites until stiff. Gradually whisk in the sugar, a spoonful at a time, whisking thoroughly between each addition. Using a spatula or large metal spoon, gently fold in the walnuts, cornflour and vinegar.

❸ Spoon the mixture in 4 piles on the prepared baking tray – leave plenty of space around each pile. Level them to form rounds, making a dip in the centre of each. Bake for 15–20 minutes until golden. They should feel firm on the surface and soft when prodded. Cool for 5 minutes before serving.

❹ Place them on individual serving plates, top with the fromage frais or yogurt and a generous spoonful of plums. Serve at once.

Pear Bread Pudding

Preparation and cooking time: 55 minutes.
Freezing: not recommended. Serves 4–6.

This takes a while to bake, but you can put it together in a flash
and let it cook away while you and your guests are enjoying dinner.
Try using apples instead of pears – or even a combination of the two.

6 slices granary bread, buttered and cut
  in fingers
2 large ripe pears, cored and sliced
125 g (4 oz) sultanas
2 large eggs

568 ml (1 pint) milk
125 g (4 oz) brown sugar
2 teaspoons cinnamon
$1/2$ teaspoon freshly grated nutmeg
custard or cream, to serve

❶ Preheat the oven to Gas Mark 4/180°C/
350°F. Grease a shallow, ovenproof dish.
❷ Lay the bread fingers, buttered side
up, in the dish. Arrange half of the sliced
pears on top of the bread and scatter
over the sultanas. Beat together the eggs,
milk and half of the sugar in a mixing
bowl. Pour this over the bread and fruit
and let soak for 10 minutes.

❸ Arrange the rest of the pears slices
over the top of the pudding and sprinkle
with the remaining sugar and the
cinnamon and nutmeg.
❹ Bake for 45–50 minutes, until the
custard is set and the top is crusty and
golden brown. Serve warm or cold with
custard or cream.

Lunches and Brunches

This selection of light dishes is perfect for a casual lunch or a lazy Sunday brunch. Many of the recipes can be adapted and used as a first course or even as a light supper dish.

Herb and Cheese Muffins

Preparation and cooking time: 35 minutes.
Freezing: not recommended. Makes 8 muffins.

These muffins are good served with any savoury dish, but they were specially created to go with the Stir-fried Beetroot with Crème Fraîche.

250 g (8 oz) plain flour
¹/₂ teaspoon salt
3¹/₂ teaspoons baking powder
2 eggs
4 tablespoons olive oil
250 ml (8 fl oz) buttermilk or full-fat milk

75 g (3 oz) parmesan or Gruyère cheese, grated
1 tablespoon chopped fresh sage
1 tablespoon chopped fresh chives
1 tablespoon chopped fresh parsley

❶ Preheat the oven to Gas Mark 5/190°C/375°F.

❷ Grease the muffin tins.

❸ Sift together the flour, salt and baking powder in a large bowl. In a separate bowl, beat together the eggs, oil and buttermilk or full-fat milk, and stir in the grated cheese and chopped herbs. Quickly mix the wet ingredients into the flour, being careful not to overstir.

❹ Spoon the batter into the greased muffin holes and bake for 20–25 minutes. Cool the muffins in the tin for a few minutes. Serve them warm.

Stir-fried Beetroot with Crème Fraîche

Preparation and cooking time: 5 minutes.
Freezing: not recommended. Serves 4.

The natural sweetness of the beetroot will come as a surprise if you're used to eating the pickled variety.

50 g (2 oz) butter
450 g (15 oz) raw beetroot, peeled and shredded

zest and juice of 1 lemon
300 ml (10 fl oz) crème fraîche, to serve
salt and freshly ground black pepper

❶ Melt the butter in a large frying pan and stir-fry the grated beetroot for 2 minutes, until very hot.

❷ Season well with the lemon zest and juice, salt and pepper. Serve at once with a dollop of crème fraîche and the warm Herb and Cheese Muffins.

Warm Sesame Chicken Salad

Preparation and cooking time: 15 minutes.
Freezing: not recommended. Serves 4.

The hot stir-fried chicken wilts the crisp salad leaves just as it is served, creating a lovely contrast of textures. This dish will be a certain success next time friends come for lunch.

2 large, skinless, boneless chicken breasts, thawed if frozen
3 tablespoons coarse-grained mustard
1 tablespoon clear honey
juice of 1 lemon
3 tablespoons sesame oil
½ tablespoon sunflower oil
1 ripe avocado
1 large bag of crisp salad greens
3 tablespoons vinaigrette
2 tablespoons sesame seeds
salt and freshly ground black pepper

1 Slice the chicken breasts into finger-sized strips. Combine the mustard, honey, lemon juice and sesame oil in a shallow dish, add the chicken and season well.

2 Heat the sunflower oil in a wok or large frying pan until very hot. Tip in the chicken and marinade and stir-fry for 5–6 minutes, or until the chicken strips are cooked.

3 Meanwhile, slice the avocado and gently toss it with the salad greens in the vinaigrette. Divide between 4 large dinner plates.

4 Add the sesame seeds to the cooked chicken and cook for 1 minute more, or until the seeds begin to change colour. Pile the hot sesame chicken and its juices over the salad leaves and serve at once.

Boston Beans

Preparation and cooking time: 25 minutes.
Freezing: not recommended. Serves 4–6.

Serve these tasty beans with garlic bread, bacon and eggs, or as a filling for jacket potatoes.

1 tablespoon olive oil
1 large onion, chopped
1 garlic clove, crushed
432 g can of pinto beans, drained
420 g can of soya beans, drained
juice of 1 lemon
400 g (13 oz) can of chopped tomatoes
550 g jar of tomato passata
2 teaspoons brown sugar
1 tablespoon coarse-grained mustard
salt and freshly ground black pepper

1 Heat the oil in a large saucepan and fry the onion until softened. Add the garlic and drained beans and fry for 2 minutes more.

2 Stir in the lemon juice, tomatoes, passata and brown sugar. Season well and bring to a boil. Simmer gently for 15 minutes, adding a little more water if necessary.

3 Stir in the mustard and serve hot.

Skillet Beef Mushrooms with Blue Cheese Dressing

Preparation and cooking time: 20 minutes.
Freezing: not recommended. Serves 2–4.

These large flat mushrooms have an excellent flavour – serve them for brunch or lunch with plenty of good bread to soak up the tasty juices.

4 very large flat mushrooms
200 ml (7 fl oz) vinaigrette
1 tablespoon coriander seeds, crushed
freshly ground black pepper
watercress or salad leaves, to garnish

For the blue cheese dressing:
175 g (6 oz) blue cheese, crumbled
5 tablespoons fromage frais
3 tablespoons orange juice
1 tablespoon coarse-grained mustard
1 teaspoon wine vinegar
salt and freshly ground black pepper

❶ Peel the mushrooms and trim the stalks. Combine the vinaigrette with the crushed coriander seeds, and season well with pepper. Pour the vinaigrette mixture over the mushrooms and set aside for 10 minutes to allow the flavours to infuse.

❷ Meanwhile, preheat the grill and make the blue cheese dressing. Blend together the dressing ingredients, using a spoon or spatula to beat the lumps out. Season to taste and transfer to a serving dish.

❸ Heat a frying pan and add the mushrooms and the vinaigrette marinade. Fry for about 2 minutes on each side, or until very brown.

❹ Place the pan under the grill for a few minutes, until the mushrooms are tender. Make sure to protect the frying pan handle from the heat.

❺ Serve the mushrooms on individual plates, garnished with watercress and a generous spoonful of the blue cheese dressing.

Hungarian Pork Goulash with Sage Dumplings

Preparation and cooking time: 50 minutes.
Freezing: recommended for goulash only. Serves 4.

These herby dumplings turn a simple goulash into a warming lunch or light supper dish. Perfect for after an autumn stroll.

2 tablespoons olive oil

750 g (1½ lb) pork fillet, cut in 2.5 cm
 (1-inch) pieces

2 large onions, chopped

1 large fennel bulb, sliced thinly

2 heaped teaspoons paprika

2 teaspoons plain flour

400 g (13 oz) can of chopped tomatoes

2 tablespoons sun-dried tomato paste

900 ml (1½ pints) vegetable stock

150 ml (¼ pint) red wine (optional –
 otherwise increase stock)

salt and freshly ground black pepper

For the herby dumplings:

50 g (2 oz) butter or margarine

175 g (6 oz) self-raising flour

75 g (3 oz) mature Cheddar cheese, grated

2 tablespoons chopped fresh sage

about 150 ml (¼ pint) cold water

salt and freshly ground black pepper

To garnish:

grated zest of 1 lemon

chopped fresh parsley

❶ Heat the oil in a large saucepan and fry the pork until lightly browned. Remove from the pan using a slotted spoon and set aside.

❷ Fry the onions and fennel in the remaining oil, until softened and golden brown. Stir in the paprika and flour and heat for 30 seconds. Return the pork to the pan and add the tomatoes, tomato paste, vegetable stock and wine (if using). Season well, bring to a boil and simmer gently for 40 minutes, adding extra stock if necessary.

❸ Fifteen minutes before serving, make the dumplings. Rub the butter into the flour, add the grated cheese, sage and salt and pepper. Stir in enough cold water to make a dough and knead gently until firm enough to form into 8 dumplings. Pop the dumplings into the goulash – they will float on the surface. Cover the goulash and simmer for 8–10 minutes, or until the dumplings are cooked.

❹ Ladle the goulash into large soup bowls and sprinkle with the lemon zest and parsley. Serve at once.

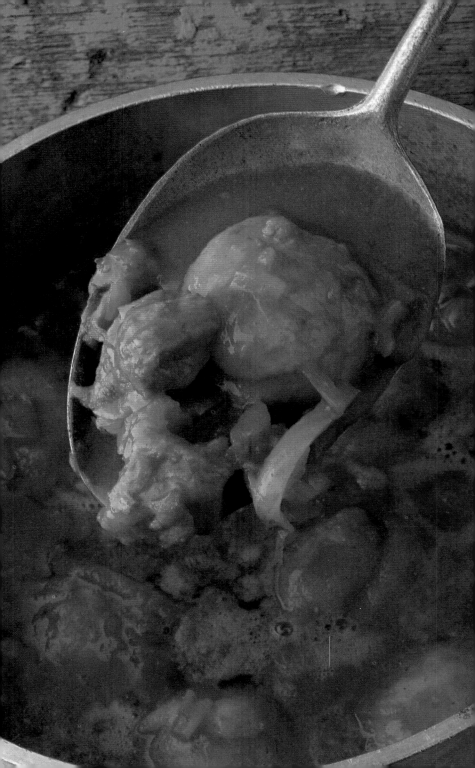

Cheesy Bubble and Squeak

Preparation and cooking time: 20 minutes.
Freezing: not recommended. Serves 4.

This is one of my family's favourites – serve it with eggs, bacon and smoked fish for Sunday brunch. It can also stand on its own as a light supper dish.

5 potatoes, cut in chunks with skins left on
2 tablespoons olive oil
3 Cox's apples, cored and sliced thickly
2 leeks, washed and shredded
1 teaspoon brown sugar
150 ml (¼ pint) vegetable stock
1 garlic clove, crushed (optional)

1 tablespoon fresh thyme leaves
juice of 1 orange
250 g (8 oz) spring greens, washed and
  shredded
150 g (5 oz) parmesan cheese, grated
salt and freshly ground black pepper

❶ Parboil the potatoes for 6–8 minutes, or until just cooked. Drain and reserve.

❷ Heat the oil in a wok or large, deep frying pan and stir-fry the chopped apples and leeks, sprinkling in the sugar and cooking over a high heat until lightly browned.

❸ Add the parboiled potatoes and fry for 1 minute more. Pour in the stock, garlic, thyme, orange juice and shredded greens. Season well.

❹ Gently toss to combine the ingredients and scatter the cheese over the top. Cover the pan and reduce the heat. Cook for 4–5 minutes, or until heated through. Serve at once with warm crusty bread.

Decorative Fruit Platter

Preparation time: 15 minutes.
Freezing: not recommended.

This is a striking way to present fresh fruit and berries – any combination can be used. You can cut the fruit ahead of time (make sure to keep it covered) and then arrange it on the crushed ice just before serving.

a selection of fresh fruits (e.g., bananas, strawberries, oranges, peaches, nectarines, kiwis, cherries, pineapple etc.)

crushed ice
juice of 1 lemon
fresh mint leaves

❶ Wash and prepare the fruits, cutting them in large, bite-sized pieces.
❷ Cover the base of your platter or serving plates with crushed ice.
❸ Arrange the fruit on the ice, sprinkle with lemon juice and a little more crushed ice.
❹ Leave to chill for 5 minutes and then garnish with the mint leaves. Serve immediately.

Peach Gratin

Preparation and cooking time: 15 minutes.
Freezing: not recommended. Serves 4.

Peaches and cream take on a sizzling new meaning with this tasty recipe.

6 very ripe peaches or 800 g (1 lb 10 oz)
   canned peaches
250 g (8 oz) strawberries, raspberries or
   redcurrants, washed and hulled (or
   stemmed)
grated zest and juice of 1 orange

284 ml (10 fl oz) double cream
125 g (4 oz) demerara sugar
$1/2$ teaspoon nutmeg
1 tablespoon cocoa powder
125 g (4 oz) flaked almonds

❶ Preheat the grill to a medium-low heat. Halve the peaches and remove the stones. Lay the peaches cut-side up in a shallow flameproof dish. Toss the berries in the orange zest and juice and spoon them into the hollows of the peach halves. Pour the cream over the top.
❷ Combine the sugar, nutmeg and cocoa powder and sprinkle over the peaches and cream.
❸ Grill for 5–6 minutes until bubbling hot. Remove from the grill and scatter the almonds over. Turn the grill to its highest setting and grill for 30 seconds, or until the flaked almonds are lightly toasted. Serve at once.

Instant Berry Ice Cream

Preparation time: 5 minutes.
Freezing: recommended. Serves 4–6.

This quick-and-easy ice cream will be an instant success. The secret is to let the berries thaw only slightly.

500 g (1 lb) frozen berries, thawed slightly
   (about 15 minutes)
250 g (8 oz) Greek-style yogurt

2–3 tablespoons icing sugar
3 tablespoons orange-flavoured liqueur
   (optional)

❶ Combine the slightly thawed berries with the yogurt, icing sugar (to taste) and liqueur (if using) in a food processor, and blend briefly until smooth.
❷ Serve at once, or cover and freeze until needed.

Casual Suppers These simple

supper dishes are as much at home at the kitchen table as at the dining table. The emphasis here is on ease of preparation, on enjoying good food and good company.

Oriental Vegetables with Spiced Noodles

Preparation and cooking time: 35 minutes.
Freezing: not recommended. Serves 4.

Cooking with a wok is one of the easiest and tastiest ways of cooking – with minimal clean-up you gain maximum taste!

1 tablespoon olive oil

1 large onion, chopped

$1/2$ teaspoon chilli powder

1 cm ($1/2$-inch) piece of fresh root
   ginger, grated

1 garlic clove, crushed

1 tablespoon chopped lemon grass

2 tablespoons unsweetened desiccated
   coconut

1 large potato, grated

3 large carrots, peeled and sliced on
   the diagonal

750 ml ($11/4$ pints) vegetable stock

250 g (8 oz) mange-tout or dwarf green
   beans

salt and freshly ground black pepper

For the spiced noodles:

250 g (8 oz) Chinese egg noodles

2 tablespoons mild curry powder

2 tablespoons crunchy peanut butter

2 tablespoons soy sauce

300 ml ($1/2$ pint) water

3 teaspoons sesame oil

250 g (8 oz) spring greens, washed
   and shredded

❶ Heat the olive oil in a large saucepan and cook the onion until softened. Add the chilli powder, ginger, garlic, lemon grass and coconut, and cook for 1 minute.
❷ Stir in the potato, carrots and stock. Season well and bring to a boil. Simmer for 10 minutes, add the mange-tout or beans and simmer for 10 minutes more.
❸ Meanwhile, 10 minutes before serving, cook the noodles according to the pack instructions. Drain. Combine the curry

powder, peanut butter, soy sauce and water in a small bowl.
❹ Heat the sesame oil in a wok and toss in the drained noodles. Heat through for 2 minutes, add the curried peanut sauce and toss well. Stir in the spring greens and cover the wok. Cook for 2 minutes longer, or until the greens are wilted.
❺ Transfer the vegetables and the spicy noodles to a large platter and serve at once.

Basil Mash with Sausages and Onion Gravy

Preparation and cooking time: 35 minutes.
Freezing: not recommended. Serves 4.

The basil adds a fresh flavour to this old favourite.

1 kg (2 lb) potatoes, chopped roughly
500 g (1 lb) sausages
50 g (2 oz) butter
300 ml (1/2 pint) milk
1 packet fresh basil, chopped finely
4 tablespoons chopped fresh parsley
salt and freshly ground black pepper
For the onion gravy:
2 tablespoons olive oil

4 large onions, sliced
1 tablespoon sugar
1 level tablespoon flour
450 ml (3/4 pint) vegetable stock
150 ml (1/4 pint) beer or red wine
1 tablespoon wine vinegar
1 tablespoon coarse-grained mustard
salt and freshly ground black pepper

❶ Boil the potatoes in salted water until tender. Drain and keep warm.

❷ Meanwhile for the gravy, heat the olive oil in a saucepan and add the onions. Cover and cook gently until very soft.

❸ Stir in the sugar. Increase the heat and fry for 2 minutes. Add the flour and stir thoroughly. Pour in the stock, beer or wine and wine vinegar. Bring to a boil and simmer for 15 minutes, adding extra stock if necessary. Stir in the mustard and seasoning a few minutes before serving.

❹ Meanwhile, cook the sausages according to the pack instructions.

❺ Mash the potatoes with the butter, milk and chopped herbs. Season to taste and serve with the sausages and gravy.

Spiced Marmalade Chicken

Preparation and cooking time: 45 minutes.
Freezing: not recommended. Serves 4.

The original Spanish recipe uses honey instead of marmalade.

3 heaped tablespoons orange marmalade
2 teaspoons ground coriander
4 teaspoons ground cumin
2 garlic cloves, crushed

3 tablespoons lemon juice
12 chicken thighs
fresh coriander, to garnish
salt and freshly ground black pepper

❶ Preheat the oven to Gas Mark 5/190°C/ 375°F.

❷ Combine the marmalade, coriander, cumin, garlic and lemon juice in a small bowl. Season well.

❸ Place the chicken pieces in a large roasting pan and spread the marmalade mixture over them.

❹ Bake the chicken for 35–40 minutes until it is cooked through. The skins should be dark and glossy and the marmalade caramelised. Transfer the chicken to a warm platter and garnish with coriander. Serve at once.

Pan-fried Chicken with Green Olives

Preparation and cooking time: 30 minutes.
Freezing: not recommended. Serves 4.

Serve this savoury chicken dish with Giant Peppered Chips (see below) and peas for a hearty casual supper.

2 tablespoons olive oil
1 large onion, chopped
3 rashers smoked lean bacon, chopped
4 boneless chicken breasts, seasoned
2 garlic cloves, crushed

300 ml (1/2 pint) red wine
12 pitted green olives
175 g (6 oz) raisins
1 bay leaf
1 sprig fresh thyme

❶ Preheat the oven to Gas Mark 5/190°C/375°F.
❷ Heat the oil in a frying pan and sauté the onion and bacon until golden brown. Add the chicken and cook for 1 minute on each side, until lightly coloured.

❸ Stir in the garlic, red wine, olives, raisins, bay leaf and sprig of thyme. Bring to a boil and then transfer the contents to an ovenproof serving dish. Bake, covered, for 20 minutes, or until the chicken is cooked through. Remove the bay leaf and serve.

Giant Peppered Chips

Preparation and cooking time: 45 minutes.
Freezing: not recommended. Serves 4.

These 'oven-fried' chips are healthier than the deep-fried variety and the seasoning makes them taste simply divine!

1 kg (2 lb) potatoes, washed but not peeled
4 tablespoons olive oil
3 tablespoons soy sauce

1 teaspoon salt
freshly ground black pepper

❶ Preheat the oven to Gas Mark 6/200°C/400°F.
❷ Cut the potatoes into very thick chips and place them on a non-stick baking tray or shallow roasting pan. Combine

the oil and soy sauce and drizzle over the potatoes. Season with plenty of salt and black pepper and toss well to coat.
❸ Bake for 40–45 minutes, turning occasionally, until golden brown and crisp.

Char-grilled Salmon with Fruit Salsa

Preparation and cooking time: 5 minutes + 30 minutes standing. Freezing: not recommended. Serves 4.

This is a delicious way of preparing salmon. Try serving it with Curried Green Lentils (page 52) as a change from the fruit salsa.

4 x 150 g (5 oz) thick salmon fillets
juice of 1 lime
1 teaspoon olive oil + extra for brushing
2 teaspoons mild chilli powder
For the fruit salsa:
4 ripe nectarines, chopped finely

½ bunch spring onions, chopped
1 green pepper, chopped finely
juice of 1 lemon or lime
2 tablespoons chopped fresh mint
1 tablespoon olive oil
salt and freshly ground black pepper

❶ Brush the salmon fillets with the lime juice and a little olive oil. Sprinkle them with the chilli powder and set aside.

❷ Meanwhile, mix together the fruit salsa ingredients in a small bowl and set aside for 30 minutes to allow the flavours to combine.

❸ Preheat the grill. Heat the teaspoon of olive oil in a frying pan until sizzling. Place the salmon fillets into the pan, flesh side down, and leave over a medium-heat for 1–2 minutes, or until very brown.

❹ Remove the pan from the heat and place it under the grill, making sure to protect the handle from the heat. Grill until the salmon skin is crispy and brown and the fish is cooked through.

❺ Invert the fish on to a warm platter and spoon the fruit salsa alongside. Serve at once.

Curried Green Lentils

Preparation and cooking time: 35 minutes.
Freezing: recommended. Serves 4.

These lentils make a great side dish for any chicken or fish recipe. They freeze well (add the crème fraîche when reheating) so you can double the quantity and save the rest for your next impromptu dinner party.

1 tablespoon olive oil

1 large onion, chopped

2 teaspoons garam masala

1 cm (1/2-inch) piece of fresh root ginger, peeled and grated

250 g (8 oz) green lentils, washed

900 ml (1¼ pint) vegetable stock

salt and freshly ground black pepper

2 tablespoons crème fraîche, to serve

❶ Heat the olive oil in a saucepan and fry the onion until just softened. Stir in the garam masala and ginger and cook for 1 minute.

❷ Add the lentils and stock, bring to a boil and simmer for 25 minutes, or until the lentils are just cooked. Add extra liquid if necessary.

❸ Stir in the crème fraîche, season to taste and transfer to a warm serving dish. Serve at once.

Lamb and Butter Bean Stew

Preparation time: 10 minutes + 40 minutes cooking.
Freezing: recommended. Serves 4.

Serve this deliciously thick stew with hunks of country-style bread and plenty of steamed vegetables.

2 tablespoons olive oil

3 large leeks, washed and shredded

500 g (1 lb) lean lamb, cubed

2 garlic cloves, crushed

1 large sprig fresh rosemary

400 g (13 oz) can of chopped tomatoes

550 g jar of tomato passata

2 x 420 g cans of butter beans, drained

300 ml (1/2 pint) beer

150 ml (1/4 pint) water

salt and freshly ground black pepper

❶ Heat the oil in a large saucepan and fry the leeks until softened and golden brown.

❷ Add the lamb and garlic and fry for 2 minutes, stirring well to brown the lamb all over. Stir in the remaining ingredients and season well.

❸ Bring to a boil and then simmer for 40 minutes, adding extra water if necessary. Season to taste and serve at once.

Open Apricot Pie

Preparation time: 5 minutes + 35 minutes baking.
Freezing: not recommended. Serves 4–6.

Ready-made pastry allows you to make beautiful home-baked pies in no time at all. Substitute rhubarb, gooseberries, cherries, peaches or plums for a change of flavour.

375 g (12 oz) ready-made shortcrust pastry, thawed if frozen

For the filling:

1 egg, separated with yolk and white each beaten

2 rounded tablespoons semolina

750 g (1½ lb) apricots, halved and stoned

75 g (3 oz) caster sugar

2 teaspoons ground cinnamon

❶ Preheat the oven to Gas Mark 6/200°C/400°F. Lightly grease a baking tray.

❷ Roll the pastry out to a 30 cm (12-inch) round on a floured surface. Transfer it to the greased baking tray, using a palette knife or fish slice. Brush the pastry base with the egg yolk and sprinkle the semolina over. This will absorb the cooking juices from the fruit.

❸ Arrange the prepared apricots on the pastry base, leaving a 5–8 cm (2–3 inch) edge. Turn up and fold over the edges of the pastry, twisting them to form a pattern. Don't worry if the pastry breaks, just patch it – the pie is meant to look rustic. Brush the pastry edges with the beaten egg white and sprinkle the entire pie with the caster sugar and cinnamon.

❹ Bake for 30–35 minutes, or until the crust is golden brown. Serve warm or cold with vanilla ice cream or custard.

A Trifle Different

Preparation time: 5 minutes + 20 minutes baking.
Freezing: not recommended. Serves 4.

The walnuts and mandarins add a delicious flavour and interesting texture to this traditional pudding.

375 g (12 oz) walnut cake, sliced

411 g can of mandarins

2 large, ripe bananas, sliced

500 ml (1 pint) thick custard, chilled

4 egg whites

250 g (8 oz) caster sugar

125 g (4 oz) chopped walnuts

❶ Preheat the oven to Gas Mark 5/190°C/ 375°F.

❷ Line the base of a large, shallow, ovenproof serving dish with the slices of walnut cake.

❸ Spoon the mandarins with their juices over the cake. Scatter the bananas on top. Pour the custard over the whole pudding and set aside.

❹ Whisk the egg whites until stiff, and gradually add the sugar one tablespoon at a time, beating well between each addition. Fold the chopped walnuts into the meringue and gently spread it over the pudding. Fluff the meringue up with a fork to form small peaks and bake for 15–20 minutes, or until golden brown. Serve at once.

Sauce-y Chocolate Pudding

Preparation time: 10 minutes + 35 minutes baking.
Freezing: not recommended. Serves 10.

This pudding really lives up to its name – be even more decadent and serve it with rich vanilla ice cream or hot custard!

125 g (4 oz) butter or margarine + extra for greasing

425 g (14 oz) caster sugar

2 eggs

300 g (10 oz) self-raising flour

4 tablespoons cocoa powder

450 ml (3/4 pint) milk

600 ml (1 pint) hot water

❶ Preheat the oven to Gas Mark 5/190°C/ 375°F. Grease a large, shallow, ovenproof dish.

❷ Cream together the butter and 250 g (8 oz) caster sugar until light and fluffy. Beat in the eggs and sift in the flour and 2 tablespoons of cocoa powder, alternating it with the milk. Combine thoroughly and pour into the prepared dish.

❸ Combine the remaining caster sugar and cocoa powder and sift this on to the pudding. Gently pour the hot water into the dish and bake for 30–35 minutes, or until the pudding has set.

❹ Let cool for a few minutes and serve with ice cream or custard.

Cooking for Crowds

Although cooking for a crowd can seem daunting, if you keep the following tips in mind you'll soon feel confident enough to invite all of your friends to dinner at once!

The menu ideas given here can be mixed and matched to suit your own tastes and numbers.

1. Always make less food than you think you'll need.

2. Keep it simple, including the presentation.

3. Be organised – work out a plan of action and tick off things as you go along.

4. For the best quality and economy, choose foods that are in season.

5. Divide your shopping list into sections: i.e., canned; dried; drink; dairy; frozen; meat and fish; fruit and vegetables. If you pick up your groceries in this order, the heavier items will be at the bottom of your trolley, preventing soft fruits and vegetables from being crushed.

6. If making only one salad, allow a fairly large portion per person; if serving a selection of salads allow only a small amount of each.

7. Allow 50–75 g (2–3 oz) of light vegetables (i.e., peas, mange-tout or beans) per person. Be slightly more generous with vegetables such as potatoes, carrots or parsnips; 150–175 g (5–6 oz) per person should be more than adequate.

8. If your guests will be standing or sitting with their plates on their laps, make sure that the food you serve can be eaten using only a fork.

9. Allow approximately half a bottle of wine per head and don't forget to have mineral water and soft drinks on hand for children and drivers.

Menu I – Rapido Feast

This is a simple, 'no cook' menu that you can assemble in minutes for any number of guests. Just add a few colourful salads, a selection of good breads, cheeses, and wine and beer to your shopping list and you'll have all the makings for a colourful and rustic feast.

This menu would also be ideal to eat *al fresco* or even to pack in a hamper for a party further afield.

platter of charcuterie – allow approximately 150 g (5 oz) of cured meat per person – including prosciutto, mortadella, pastrami, smoked turkey, salami and Parma ham

fresh watercress and wedges of ripe melon, to garnish

selection of mustards and pickles

selection of antipasto – a good variety of prepared vegetable antipasto is available in jars; mushrooms, artichokes, peppers etc. Drain off some of the oil and use it for cooking or salad dressings.

Green and Black Olives in Pistou (page 6)

ready prepared hummus, taramasalata and tzatiki

Decorative Fruit Platter (page 40)

Menu II
For 12–15 people

Chicken with Apricots and Spiced Croûtes
Warm Baked Brie with Plum Compote
Pastarocca
Caramelised Citrus Apple Tart

Chicken with Apricots

Preparation time: 10 minutes + 40–45 minutes cooking.
Freezing: recommended. Serves 12–15.

This dish can also be made with prunes instead of apricots.

3 tablespoons olive oil

3 large onions, sliced

24 skinless, boneless chicken thighs, halved

6 garlic cloves, crushed

6 large carrots, peeled and chopped

4 celery sticks, chopped

1 packet fresh rosemary

2 bay leaves

1 kg (2 lb) ready-to-eat apricots

4 tablespoons flour

2.25 litres (4 pints) chicken stock

1 bottle Spanish red wine

salt and freshly ground black pepper

chopped fresh parsley, to garnish

❶ Heat the oil in a large saucepan and fry the onions until softened. Add the chicken and brown for 5 minutes, stirring occasionally.

❷ Add the garlic, carrots, celery, herbs and apricots. Sprinkle in the flour, stir and cook for 2 minutes more. Pour in the stock and wine and bring to a boil. Simmer gently for 45–50 minutes, or until the chicken is cooked through. Season to taste.

❸ Transfer to a warm serving platter and scatter with chopped parsley and Spiced Croûtes (see below).

Spiced Croûtes

Preparation and cooking time: 10 minutes.
Freezing: not recommended. Serves 12–15.

You can make these ahead and keep them warm in the oven.

125 g (4 oz) butter

150 ml (¼ pint) olive oil

2 teaspoons chilli powder

2 teaspoons ground cumin

1 teaspoon ground coriander

1 large french stick, cut in 1 cm (½-inch) slices

❶ Heat the butter and olive oil in a large frying pan. Mix the spices together and stir them into the hot oil. Add the sliced bread and fry for 1 minute on each side, or until golden brown.

❷ Keep warm in the oven until needed.

Pastarocca

Preparation time: 10 minutes + 30–35 minutes cooking.
Freezing: not recommended. Serves 12–15.

As feta cheese is quite salty, this dish needs little seasoning.

3 tablespoons olive oil
3 garlic cloves, crushed
750 g (1½ lb) dried spinach and wholewheat
  pasta shapes, cooked and drained
3 tablespoons chopped fresh thyme
750 g (1½ lb) spring greens, shredded
  and parboiled

1.25 kg (3 lb) potatoes, cooked and chopped
  roughly
750 g (1½ lb) feta cheese
1.25 litres (2¼ pints) double cream
250 g (8 oz) parmesan cheese, crumbled
250 g (8 oz) fresh breadcrumbs
freshly ground black pepper

❶ Preheat the oven to Gas Mark 6/200°C/ 400°F. Grease 2 large, shallow, ovenproof dishes with the olive oil.

❷ In a large bowl, gently mix together the garlic, cooked pasta, thyme, spring greens, potatoes and feta cheese. Season with plenty of pepper.

❸ Divide the mixture between the prepared dishes.

❹ Pour the cream equally into both dishes and sprinkle on the parmesan cheese and breadcrumbs. Bake for 30–35 minutes until golden brown and bubbly on top. Let cool for a few minutes before serving.

Warm Baked Brie with Plum Compote

Preparation and cooking time: 30 minutes.
Freezing: not recommended. Serves 10–12.

You can use store-bought apricot jam instead of the plum compote.

1 kg (2 lb) Brie cheese
freshly ground black pepper
For the plum compote:
1 kg (2 lb) plums, halved and stoned

25 g (1 oz) butter
125 g (4 oz) brown sugar
1 teaspoon ground cinnamon
juice and rind of 1 orange

❶ To make the compote, simmer all the ingredients in a covered saucepan for 5 minutes. Remove the lid and simmer for 8–10 minutes more until the plums are just soft. Cool slightly.

❷ Preheat the oven to Gas Mark 6/200°C/ 400°F.

❸ Place the Brie in a shallow, ovenproof serving dish. Season well with black pepper and spoon on the compote.

❹ Bake for 8–12 minutes or until the Brie is warm and very soft.

❺ Serve at once with warm oatcakes or crusty bread.

Caramelised Citrus Apple Tart

Preparation time: 10 minutes + 35–40 minutes baking.
Freezing: not recommended. Serves 12.

This is a wonderfully novel but simple version of the traditional apple pie. Try using pears instead of apples as an interesting alternative.

500 g (1 lb) puff pastry, thawed if frozen
3 teaspoons ground cinnamon
175 g (6 oz) caster sugar
6 large dessert apples, cored and sliced
  thinly

2 tablespoons dried breadcrumbs
150 g (5 oz) butter
grated zest of 2 lemons and 2 oranges
icing sugar, to dust

❶ Preheat the oven to Gas Mark 6/200°C/400°F.

❷ Roll the puff pastry dough out in a large round, 3 mm (1/8-inch) thick, and sprinkle with the cinnamon and half of the caster sugar.

❸ Scatter one-quarter of the apple slices over the pastry, leaving a 5 cm (2-inch) edge. Sprinkle with the breadcrumbs and a little more caster sugar.

❹ Arrange the remaining apple slices in concentric circles, beginning from the outside edge and overlapping the slices towards the centre of the tart. Lift the pastry edge and fold it over, pinching it to seal and form a rim.

❺ Sprinkle with the remaining sugar and dot with the butter and lemon and orange zest. Bake for 35–40 minutes, or until the tart is brown and crisp and the apples are tender. Check the tart half-way through the cooking time. If the pastry is already browned, cover the edges with foil and continue to bake.

❻ Allow to cool for a few minutes and then, using a fish slice or palette knife, slide the tart on to a large platter or chopping board. Dust with icing sugar and cut in wedges. Serve warm with custard or Greek-style yogurt.

Menu III
For 12 people
Aubergine and Pepper Relish
Spanish Vegetable Stew with Picada
Roasted New Potatoes with Thyme
Chestnut Chocolate Cake

Aubergine and Pepper Relish

Preparation and cooking time: 30 minutes.
Freezing: not recommended. Serves 12.

Serve this savoury relish with warm crusty bread and a warning to your guests to leave room for the main course!

150 ml (¼ pint) virgin olive oil

2 large Spanish onions, chopped

4 large aubergines, diced finely

4 garlic cloves, chopped

1 bay leaf

200 ml (7 fl oz) white wine

3 sun-dried tomatoes, chopped finely

juice of 3 lemons

3 large red peppers, halved, cored and
   quartered

3 tablespoons chopped fresh coriander

salt and freshly ground black pepper

fresh coriander leaves, to garnish

❶ Heat half of the olive oil in a large frying pan or wok. Fry the onions until softened and golden brown. Add the diced aubergine, garlic and bay leaf and cook, stirring often, until the aubergine has softened and is lightly coloured.

❷ Pour in the wine, sun-dried tomatoes and lemon juice. Season well and cover. Simmer for 8–10 minutes, stirring frequently. Remove the lid and cook for 2–3 minutes more, adding a little extra wine if necessary.

❸ Meanwhile, preheat the grill and place the pepper quarters on a baking tray,

with their skins facing up. Grill the peppers until the skins are blackened. When cool enough to handle, peel off the blackened skins and cut the peppers into slivers.

❹ Remove the aubergine mixture from the heat and cool slightly. Stir in the chopped coriander and the remaining olive oil. Season to taste.

❺ Spoon the aubergine on to a large serving platter or shallow bowl. Decorate with the slivers of pepper and garnish with the coriander leaves. Serve with warm, crusty bread.

Spanish Vegetable Stew with Picada

Preparation and cooking time: 40 minutes.
Freezing: not recommended. Serves 12.

Picada is a savoury paste used in Spain to thicken and flavour stews and soups. It usually contains garlic, breadcrumbs, parsley and toasted nuts, and is traditionally made using a mortar and pestle. This quick-and-easy version uses a food processor – but the taste is just as good!

3 litres (3½ pints) water
150 ml (¼ pint) white wine
1 bay leaf
4 teaspoons cumin seeds
500 g (1 lb) carrots, peeled and sliced
4 dessert apples or pears, cored and cut in chunks
250 g (8 oz) mange-tout, topped and tailed
250 g (8 oz) french beans, topped, tailed and halved
420 g can of flageolet beans, drained
420 g can of chick peas, drained
250 g (8 oz) frozen petit pois
salt and freshly ground black pepper
For the picada:
125 g (4 oz) hazelnuts, toasted
50 g (2 oz) pinenuts, toasted
2 thick slices of day-old bread, cubed and fried in olive oil
2 large garlic cloves, crushed
a handful of fresh parsley
To garnish:
paprika
chopped fresh parsley

❶ Bring the water, wine, bay leaf and cumin seeds to a boil in a very large saucepan. Season with salt and stir in the carrots and chopped apples or pears. Simmer for 7–8 minutes.

❷ Add the mange-tout, french beans, flageolet beans, chick peas and petit pois, and simmer for 6 minutes more, or until the vegetables are just tender.

❸ Meanwhile, make the picada. Grind the nuts in a food processor or liquidiser.

Add the fried bread cubes, garlic and parsley, and process until the ingredients form a paste. Thin the paste by adding a few drops of the liquid from the vegetable stew.

❹ Stir the picada into the stew and simmer for 4–5 minutes, adding a little water if necessary. Season to taste.

❺ Serve the stew in large, warm soup bowls, garnished with a sprinkling of paprika and some chopped fresh parsley.

Roasted New Potatoes with Thyme

Preparation time: 12 minutes + 35 minutes cooking.
Freezing: not recommended. Serves 12.

Roasted new potatoes are a super accompaniment for any stew. Don't bother peeling them – most of the skin will come off with a good scrubbing, and any remaining skin simply adds an appealing texture and colour to the dish.

1.75 kg (4 lb) small new potatoes, scrubbed
6 tablespoons olive oil

salt and freshly ground black pepper
1 packet of fresh thyme, to serve

❶ Preheat the oven to Gas Mark 6/200°C/ 400°F. Parboil the potatoes in salted water for 10 minutes. Drain.

❷ Place the potatoes in a large, shallow roasting pan. Drizzle the olive oil over them, season with plenty of salt and pepper and toss them well to coat.

❸ Roast the potatoes for 30–35 minutes, or until golden brown and cooked through.

❹ Pull off the leaves from the sprigs of thyme and toss them with the hot roasted potatoes. Serve at once.

Chestnut Chocolate Cake

**Preparation and cooking time: 30 minutes + chilling.
Freezing: not recommended. Serves 12.**

This decadent pudding is the perfect finish to any dinner.

**800 g (1 lb 10 oz) canned unsweetened
chestnut purée**
3 teaspoons vanilla essence
25–50 g (1–2 oz) icing sugar, to taste
500 g (1 lb) sponge biscuit fingers
12 tablespoons dark rum or sherry
568 ml (1 pint) double cream, whipped lightly

1 tablespoon cocoa powder
375 g (12 oz) plain chocolate
50 g (2 oz) butter
2 tablespoons water
**500 g (1 lb) strawberries, washed and
left whole**
icing sugar, to decorate

❶ Beat together the chestnut purée, vanilla essence and icing sugar (to taste) until smooth. Set aside.

❷ Briefly dip enough sponge fingers in the rum or sherry (they should not be soggy) to line the base of a 30 cm (12-inch) springform cake tin.

❸ Spread half of the chestnut purée over the sponge fingers and top with half of the whipped cream. Sift a thin layer of cocoa powder over the cream, and repeat the layers, ending with a layer of sponge fingers.

❹ Melt the chocolate and butter over a low heat and stir in the water until smooth. Pour this over the biscuit top and spread to the edges, using a palette knife or spatula. Refrigerate for 2 hours (or overnight), until the chocolate is set and the cake is chilled through.

❺ Remove the sides of the springform tin and transfer the cake to a large plate or scrubbed chopping board. Gently lay 5 long thin strips of greaseproof paper on the cake's surface. Sift a thin layer of icing sugar over the top, and then remove the strips to reveal a striped pattern. Alternatively, simply seive a thin layer of icing sugar over the entire surface. Top the cake with strawberries and serve.

Finishing Touches

Although cooking for friends should be quick and easy, it is nice to add those little extra touches which turn a normal meal into a bit of an occasion. Using the following ideas, you can make any meal special, in no time at all.

NIBBLES AND BITES

On those days when you don't even have the time to put together a tray of nibbles, don't despair – there are many exciting things to be found on the supermarket shelves. Stock your cupboard with spicy corn chips, cheese straws and sesame crackers to accompany jars of salsa and pesto. Or buy fresh hummus and taramasalata and serve them with pitta or crackers and ready prepared fresh vegetables. Other tasty options are black or green olive paste (delicious on toast) and tahini paste (try it on crunchy sesame crackers).

The following recipe ideas will come in handy when you've got a few minutes to spare.

DIPS AND SPREADS

Use a food processor for amazingly speedy results. Serve as dips or spread on thick slices of garlic toast.

Flageolet Garlic Purée: Combine 1 can of drained flageolet beans with a garlic clove and 6 tablespoons of olive oil. Season well and process until smooth.

Butter Bean and Lime Purée: Take 1 can of drained butter beans, 6 tablespoons of olive oil, the juice and zest of 1–2 limes and a drop of tabasco sauce to taste. Blend together, adding a little water (or butter bean juice) if the purée is too thick.

SALSAS

A salsa is simply an uncooked sauce or relish make from finely chopped fruits and/or vegetables, flavoured with herbs, vinegar and olive oil.

Fast Tomato Salsa: Mix together equal quantities of finely chopped tomatoes (canned or fresh), spring onions and red pepper. Add plenty of crushed garlic, lime juice or vinegar, a pinch of sugar and a little olive oil. Stir in a handful of chopped fresh coriander and season with salt and freshly ground black pepper to taste. Let stand for 30 minutes to develop the flavours.

PESTOS AND FLAVOURED OILS

Traditional pesto is a paste made from basil, pine kernels, garlic, olive oil and parmesan. However, you can change a few ingredients and come up with an entirely new flavour. Look out for the ready-prepared varieties and try them tossed with steamed or grilled vegetables. They are also good stirred into soups or stews just before serving. Pestos can be drizzled over risottos or savoury rice dishes just before serving, mixed in with salad dressings or mayonnaise, or simply served in small bowls in place of butter.

Light Pesto: Blend together 150 ml (1/4 pint) virgin olive oil with a couple of handfuls of fresh parsley and coriander, 50 g (2 oz) of chopped roasted walnuts, some crushed garlic and freshly ground black pepper.

Sun-dried Tomato Pesto: Blend together 150 ml (1/4 pint) virgin olive oil with 2 tablespoons sun-dried tomato paste, a finely chopped fresh chilli and some chopped fresh thyme. Season to taste.

Simple Mixed Herb Pesto: Combine 150 ml (1/4 pint) virgin olive oil with a few handfuls of any mixture of fresh chopped herbs, the grated zest and juice of 1 lemon, and some black pepper.

FLAVOURED BUTTER AND MAYONNAISE

Use these to enhance those dishes where you would normally use plain butter or mayonnaise. Try making scrambled eggs or an omelette using parsley or dill butter. It is also delicious melted over freshly cooked vegetables – especially corn-on-the-cob or globe artichokes. Simply beat unsalted butter until soft, and flavour with the herbs of your choice. Ginger, chillis or olive or tomato tapenade also make great flavourings for butter.

Lime-flavoured mayonnaise is especially good with chips (see page 48) or with a plate of grilled vegetables or char-grilled fish. Spicy pepper and garlic-flavoured mayonnaise tastes great with grilled meats or baked potatoes. Use a mustard and apple-flavoured mayonnaise to make a pasta or potato salad. The ideas are endless.

Citrus Mayonnaise: Beat together French mayonnaise with grated lemon or lime zest and juice. Try chopped lemon grass for a more exotic flavour.

Pepper and Garlic Mayonnaise: Drain off the oil from a jar of antipasto peppers and blend with 5 tablespoons of French mayonnaise, plenty of crushed garlic, and salt and freshly ground black pepper.

Apple and Mustard Mayonnaise: Combine a few teaspoons of coarse-grained or Dijon mustard with French mayonnaise and some shredded apple. Add a dash of lemon juice and seasoning to taste.

BREADS

Serve olive bread, walnut bread, onion bread or sun-dried tomato bread alongside soups, salads and stews. Or take a plain farmhouse loaf, french stick or pizza base, and jazz it up in the blink of an eye. And don't forget croissants – delicious at breakfast, they are even better when glazed with beaten egg, sprinkled with poppy seeds and toasted in the oven to be served in place of dinner rolls.

Rustic Toast: Toast thick slices of white farmhouse bread and rub one side of each with a peeled and bruised garlic clove. Season with a sprinkling of salt and pepper and drizzle over some virgin olive oil. Serve warm.

Stuffed and Wrapped Baked Bread: Cut a french stick or ciabatta loaf in 2.5 cm (1-inch) slices, leaving the slices attached to the loaf. Mix together some olive oil, crushed garlic and anchovies (or basil, if preferred) and spread between the slices. Season with freshly ground black pepper and wrap tightly with kitchen foil. Bake in a preheated hot oven for 15–20 minutes.

Flat Pepper Bread: Brush the base of a large, prepared pizza base with plenty of virgin olive oil. Spoon on a jar of antipasto mixed peppers and drained antipasto artichokes. Season well with salt and freshly ground black pepper and bake in a preheated oven (Gas Mark 7/220°C/ 425°F) for about 15 minutes. Garnish with chopped parsley and cut in thick wedges.

SALADS

Salads are easy to 'jazz up', and with ready prepared greens, they can be put together in an instant. Try enhancing a bottled dressing with a splash of flavoured oil or some chopped fresh herbs. Or add some toasted nuts and croûtons to give a delicious texture and flavour to any salad. Try sunflower seeds with a spinach, bacon and avocado salad. Toasted pine kernels go well with watercress, raisins and radicchio, while hot spiced croûtons are just the thing with crisp Cos lettuce and feta cheese.

SOUPS

Ready-prepared soups are also easy to make a little more special. Just before serving, swirl a dollop of crème fraîche or a flavoured pesto in each bowl, and scatter some fresh chopped herbs or a sprinkling of fresh nutmeg or black pepper on top. Float some toasted bread croûtes on top with a spoonful of freshly grated parmesan cheese. You can also use ready-prepared puff pastry to make fresh croûtes. Cut small shapes (mini stars, hearts and half moons) out of pastry trimmings, brush them with egg, sprinkle with poppy seeds and bake for 8–10 minutes in a very hot oven.

Puff Pastry Soup Lids: Half-fill ovenproof soup bowls with cold soup. Roll out circles of ready-made puff pastry (thawed if frozen) just larger than the rim of your soup bowls. Brush the edges of the pastry with a little beaten egg and place the pastry lids over the soup bowls, pressing down to crimp and seal. Brush the pastry lids with the remaining beaten egg and refrigerate. When chilled, place the bowls on a baking tray and bake in a very hot oven for 15–20 minutes, until the pastry is browned and the soup is hot.

PUDDINGS

Sometimes a sticky or sweet pudding seems like too much trouble but fresh fruit isn't quite special enough for the occasion. This is when a bottle of bubbly comes in handy! Half fill some champagne glasses with soft fruits such as raspberries, strawberries or chopped peaches, and top with an inexpensive sparking wine. Very elegant and fun too.

Sweeten up fresh fruit by dipping apricots and pear slices in melted bitter chocolate. (Leave to set at room temperature and serve in paper cases.) Strawberries, physalis and seedless grapes can be treated the same way – try using a combination of white and plain chocolate.

For a final special touch at the end of a meal, serve your coffee flavoured with a split vanilla pod or lightly crushed cardamom pods. (Remember to strain the coffee before serving!) Top with a dollop of fresh cream and a sprinkling of cocoa powder or cinnamon.

Index

WARFARE AT SEA, 1500–1650

WARFARE AND HISTORY
General editor Jeremy Black
Professor of History, University of Exeter